Christmas
Themed
JOKES

For Men

CONTENTS

Ho, ho, ho, better put that hot chocolate down before these jokes make you spill your drink!

What do you get
if you cross
a snowman
and a vampire?

Frostbite!

What says
Oh, Oh, Oh?

Santa walking
backward!

Why was the
snowman looking
through the carrots?

He was
picking his
nose!

How does a snowman get around?

By riding an "icicle!"

Why did
Santa's helper
see the
psychiatrist?

Because he
had a low
"elf" esteem!

Why did the Christmas tree go to the barber?

It needed a trim!

What do you call Santa when he gets stuck in the chimney?

Claus-
trophobic!

What do you call Father Christmas on the beach?

Sandy Claus!

What do elves post on social media?

Elf-ies!

What do you call an obnoxious reindeer?

RUDE-olph!

What do snowmen eat for breakfast?

Ice Crispies!

What do Mexican sheep say at Christmas time?

¡Navidad!
Fleece

What do you call
a cat on the
beach during
Christmas time?

Sandy Claws!

What do you
call a snowman
with a six-pack?

An
abdominal
snowman!

Why did the snowman
win the Christmas
talent show?

Because he was
outstanding
in his field!

What do you call
Santa's little helpers?

Subordinate
Clauses!

What do you get when you cross a bell with a skunk?

Jingle Smells!

Why did the elf push
his bed into the
fireplace?

He wanted
to sleep
like a log!

What kind of music do elves love the most?

Wrap music!

Why did Santa's workshop get shut down by the health department?

For elf and safety reasons!

What do you call a bankrupt Santa?

Saint Nickel-less!

Why did the gingerbread man go to the doctor?

He felt crumby!

What do you call a
snowman with a
temper?

Melt-down!

Why did the
elf go to
school?

To learn his
"elf"-abet!

How do Christmas trees access the internet?

They log in!

Why did the man put
his wallet in the
freezer?

He wanted
cold hard
cash for
Christmas
shopping!

Why did the man
think the Christmas
tree was knitting?

It kept
dropping its
needles!

What did the man say
when he bought
a pair of socks
for Christmas?

"These are
stocking
stuffer
material!"

Why did the man
sit on the
Christmas lights?

He wanted
to get a little
sparkle in his
life!

How do you scare a snowman?

With a hair
dryer.

How do men prepare
their Christmas gifts?

By buying
gift bags
(wrapping)
is too
complicated).

What do snowmen eat for breakfast?

Frosted flakes!

What do snowmen call their kids?

Chill-dren!

What did the snowman say to the customer?

Have an
ice day!

Why did the snowman scream?

Because the snowblower was coming down the street!

What do snowmen wear on their heads?

Ice caps!

Where do snowmen keep their money?

In a
snowbank!

What's a snowman's favorite greens?

Iceberg
lettuce
sandwiches!

Why did Santa go to music school?

He wanted
to improve
his wrapping
skills!

What did Santa say to the smoker?

"Please don't smoke, it's bad for my ELF!"

What do you call Santa when he takes a break?

Santa Pause!

What do you call an old snowman?

Water!

Why is a Christmas
tree a must for a
party?

Because it
always lights
up the room!

What do reindeer hang on their Christmas trees?

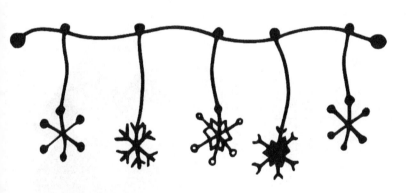

Horn-aments!

What's a reindeer's favorite game?

Stable-tennis!

KNOCK KNOCK JOKES

Hello, is anybody home? You'll want to be here for these knock-knock jokes?

Knock, knock.

Who's there?

Holly.

Holly who?

Holly-days are here again!

Knock, knock.

Who's there?

Mary.

Mary who?

Mary
Christmas!

Knock, knock.

Who's there?

Snow.

Snow who?

Snow place like home
for the holidays!

Knock, knock.

Who's there?

Yule.

Yule who?

Yule never guess
what I got you for
Christmas!

Knock, knock.

Who's there?

Donut.

Donut who?

Donut open
your gifts until
Christmas
morning!

Knock, knock.

Who's there?

Sleigh.

Sleigh who?

Sleigh my name, sleigh my name!

Knock, knock.

Who's there?

Alpaca.

Alpaca who?

Alpaca the
presents,
you bring
the tree!

Knock, knock.

Who's there?

Pudding.

Pudding who?

Pudding up the
Christmas lights takes
forever!

Knock, knock.

Who's there?

Cocoa.

Cocoa who?

Cocoa-ld outside, so let's drink some hot chocolate!

FUNNY IDEAS

Looking for something to spice up the season? Try these wild ideas to spread holiday cheer!

Candy Cane Javelin:

The goal is to throw a candy cane and make it stick upright in the snow.

Christmas Tree Limbo:

How low can you go without getting tinsel in your hair?

Gift Wrap Relay:

Race to wrap presents, but instead of tape, use spaghetti!

Twinkling Light Tag:

Turn off all the
lights, and play tag
with only twinkling
Christmas lights
to guide you.

Icicle Dueling:

Two participants, each with an icicle, try to melt the other's icicle first using just their breath.

TONGUE TWISTERS

Put that candy cane down and give your tongue a workout with these holiday themed twisters!

Santa's sleigh slides
silently southward.

Frosty's fingers find
frozen fir trees.

Ten tiny tin trains
toot ten times.

Crisp Christmas
cookies kept in
crystal containers.

Sleigh bells
sing songs
so sweetly.

Gingerbread guys give
great glee.

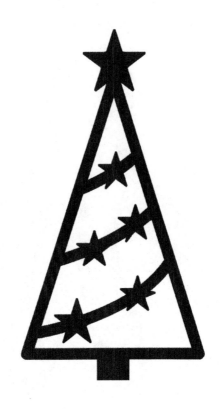

Tinsel twinkles to the
top of the tree.

Five festive fairies flit
freely forward.

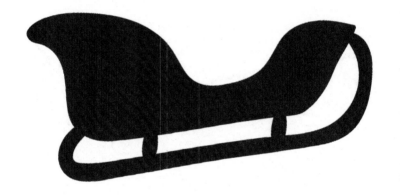

Snowflakes stick on
slick sleds.

Holly hangs
heavily in
happy houses.

Elves eagerly envelope
every elegant
evergreen.

SILLY STORIES

What holiday faux pas have you committed? See how they stack up compared to some of these…

This Christmas, I'm giving out batteries as gifts with a note: "Toys not included."

I'm writing a book for Christmas: "How to Decorate a Tree". So far, the introduction is: "Needle-little help?"

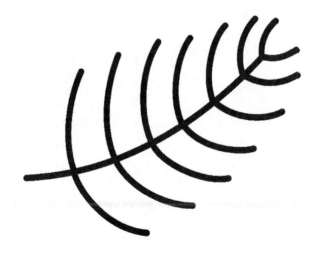

My wife asked for
something sparkling
for Christmas,
so I got her...

A bottle of window
cleaner!

My wife said she
wanted something
golden for Christmas,
so I got her...

A goldfish!

My wife wanted
diamonds for
Christmas,
so I got her...

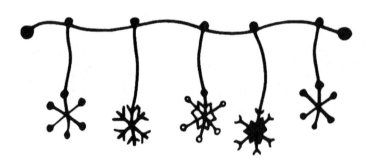

A deck of cards!

One Christmas, an elf
asked a reindeer,
"Do you know why
Santa takes an
umbrella with him on
Christmas Eve?"

The reindeer replied,
"No, why?"

The elf chuckled,
"Because of the rain,
dear!"

An elf went to a shoe
store and asked for
a pair of shoes,
but with a twist.
The shopkeeper
was puzzled.
"A twist?" he asked.

The elf replied, "Yes,
curly toes, please.
It's the latest in
elf-fashion!"

RIDDLES

Get ready to stretch your brains with these puzzling riddles to chew on!

What travels around
the world but always
stays in one corner?

A stamp on a
Christmas
card.

What's as big as Santa but weighs much less?

Santa's shadow.

I have needles but
can't sew. Who am I?

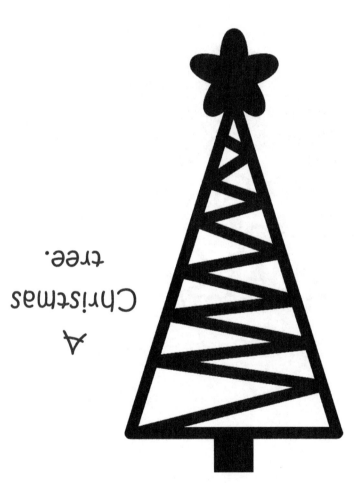

A Christmas tree.

I kiss the Earth and make it pure, yet hide the life that will endure. Who am I?

Snow.

I'm not a tree or a star overhead, but every December I'm very well-read.
Who am I?

A Christmas card.

I'm white but not a
ghost, I fall but never
hurt. Who am I?

·mouS

What did one plate say to another during Christmas dinner?

"Lunch is on me."

What did the Christmas tree say to the ornament?

"Quit hanging around!"

What did the big
candle say to the
little candle at the
family Christmas
gathering?

"I'm so
scared of
going out
tonight!"

What did the stamp say to the Christmas card?

Stick with me
and we'll go
places!

What did one snowflake say to the other snowflake?

"You're one of a kind!"

How does Christmas Day end?

With a Y!

Printed in Great Britain
by Amazon